WE'RE NOT W████

Structure and Function in the Animal Kingdom

MICHAEL GARLAND

 HOLIDAY HOUSE · NEW YORK

We're not weird. Animals need food, air, and water to live. We need to move to get these things. We need to move away from predators. We have special body parts to help us.

My large nose keeps out
dust and helps me breathe.
I am a **saiga antelope.**

I build a web to capture prey. I protect myself with my long spines. I am a female **long-horned orb-weaver spider.**

I use my tentacles to catch little fish and other prey to eat. I am an **Atolla jellyfish.**

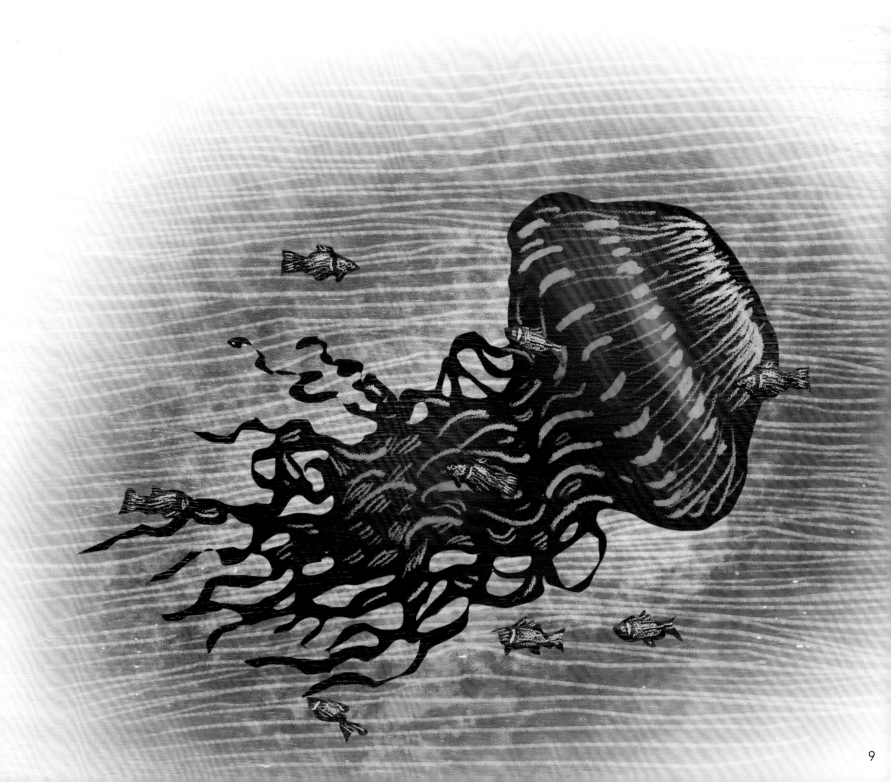

I am a fish. Like other fish, I can breathe with my gills. I can also breathe through my skin. I can swim in water, but I can also walk on land.

My front fins work like legs so I can move from one tidal pond to another to find food or escape predators. I am a **mudskipper.**

My long skinny snout has more than a hundred sharp teeth. I use it to catch fish and other prey. I am a **gharial.**

I am almost blind, but my special nose has twenty-two feelers. My feelers help me figure out where I am and help me find food like worms and insects. I am a **star-nosed mole.**

Like birds, I lay eggs and have a bill.
But I am not a bird. I am a mammal.
Birds have feathers, but like other
mammals, I have fur. My bill is
electro-sensitive to help me find
food such as crayfish and
shrimp. My webbed feet
help me swim.
I am a **platypus.**

I am a **maned wolf.** I am in the same family as wolves and other dogs, but despite my name, I am not a true wolf. My long legs help me move around quickly in the tall grass as I hunt for wild guinea pigs and rabbits.

My soft flesh lets me float close to the ocean floor where I can just wait for my dinner to come to me.

When I am brought from the bottom of the ocean to the surface, the change in pressure turns me into a soft blob that gives me my name. I am a **blobfish.**

People call me the unicorn of the sea, but my horn is really a tusk or a giant tooth. Scientists are not sure what I use it for. People think I use it to sense my surroundings, communicate with other narwhals, and stun fish to make them easier to eat. I am a **narwhal.**

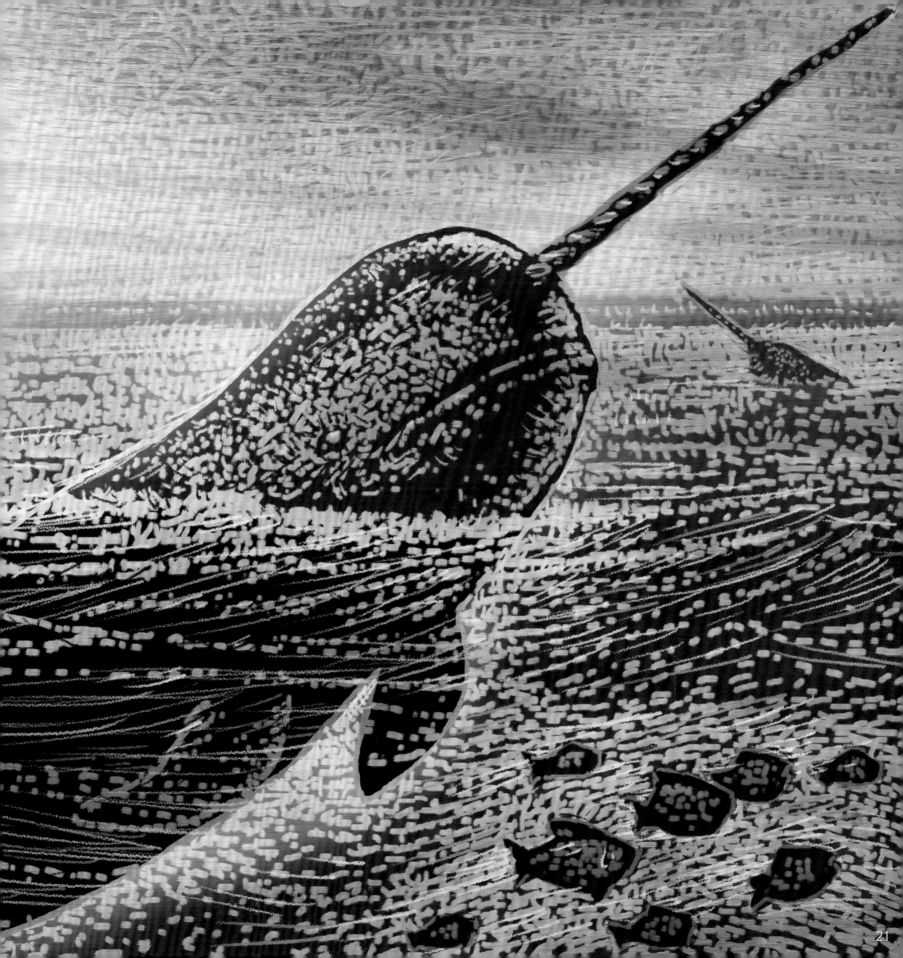

My long tongue is
perfect for eating ants.

When I feel threatened, I roll myself into a ball. Hard scales protect me from predators. I am a **pangolin.**

The rainforest is my home. I look like a kite gliding from tree to tree in the night. The skin that stretches along my body and limbs, from fingers to toes, helps me sail through the air to find food as well as places to hide from predators. I am a **Sunda flying lemur.**

I look like a zebra from the back and a deer from the front. But I am neither. My stripes and brown color camouflage me in the bush so I can stay safe from leopards, servals, and golden cats that might want to eat me. I am an **okapi.**

I have spikes on my head and the rest of my body to protect me from foxes, bobcats, snakes, and falcons.

I use my skin to collect water, which helps me survive in the hot, dry desert where I live. I am a lizard known as the **thorny dragon.**

I have a hard shell and I can retract my head and legs to shield myself from predators. I can go a long time without water because I can store it in my bladder. I am a **desert tortoise.**

I use my long proboscis and tongue to drink nectar from flowers. I look like a hummingbird, but I am an insect. I am a **hummingbird hawk-moth.**

I hope to attract a mate. That's why I dance and show off my bright blue webbed feet. I am a **blue-footed booby.**

That's not a big red balloon.
It's my inflatable sac. I use
it to charm a female. I am a
male **frigatebird.**

I have large tusks, but I don't use them for fighting. I stand on my hind legs and box when battling with rivals for a mate. I am a male **babirusa.**

I blow up my vocal sac to sing and get a mate. I can change from green to brown to gray to match my surroundings and hide from predators. I am a **gray treefrog.**

We're not weird.
Our special body parts
help us survive and thrive.

The **Atolla jellyfish** (*Atolla wyvillei*) can be found in oceans throughout the world. This jellyfish has twenty marginal tentacles and a singular large one for capturing prey such as small fish. Jellyfish are not fish; they are Scyphozoa.

The **babirusa** (*Babyrousa* spp.) lives in the jungle on the Indonesian Islands. It is sometimes called the deer-pig. It eats fruit, leaves, mushrooms, insects, fish, and small animals.

The **blobfish** (*Psychrolutes marcidus*) swims in the deep seas off the coast of Australia and New Zealand. Its blobby mass allows it to float effortlessly under the extreme pressure of the great depth. It eats mollusks, crabs, and other prey.

The **blue-footed booby** (*Sula nebouxii*) is a marine bird that lives in the subtropical and tropical eastern Pacific Ocean. It uses its bright blue feet to attract a mate. It eats fish and squid.

The **desert tortoise** (*Gopherus agassizii*) lives in the Mojave and Sonoran Deserts of the southwestern United States and Northern Mexico. It eats grasses, cactus, and wildflowers.

The **frigatebird** (*Fregata magnificens*) is a marine bird that lives in the subtropical and tropical oceans across the world. It eats fish, squid, jellyfish, and sometimes small turtles.

The **gharial** (*Gavialis gangeticus*) is a fish-eating crocodilian with a distinctive long, thin, tooth-lined snout. Its range is the Indian subcontinent.

The **gray treefrog** (*Dryophytes versicolor*) lives in the forest and lowlands of the eastern United States and southeastern Canada. It can change its color to hide from predators. It eats insects, snails, and slugs.

The **hummingbird hawk-moth** (*Macroglossum stellatarum*) is a species of moth with a long proboscis. It hums and hovers like a hummingbird when feeding on the nectar of flowers. It can be found in Europe, Northern Africa, Asia, and the Far East.

The **long-horned orb-weaver spider** (*Macracantha arcuata*) is found in tropical Eurasia. It makes a round web from sticky and non-sticky silk to catch insects for food.

The **maned wolf** (*Chrysocyon brachyurus*) is found in South America, the largest member of the dog family on the continent. It eats fruits and vegetables as well as rodents and insects.

The **mudskipper** or walking fish (*Periophthalmus* spp.) is an amphibious fish that lives in intertidal lands. It uses its pectoral or pelvic fins to walk on land. It can be found in Asia, the Far East, and Australia.

The **narwhal** (*Monodon monoceros*) lives in the Arctic seas. The male narwhal has a long tusk-like tooth that may be used to communicate or attract a mate. It eats fish, shrimp, and crabs.

The **okapi** (*Okapi johnstoni*) home range is in central Africa. It eats a variety of vegetation, including leaves, fruit, grass, and twigs. Although it has zebra-like stripes, it is closely related to the giraffe.

The **pangolin** (*Phataginus* spp.) is a family of three mammals with armor-like scales protecting their skin. They are threatened because of loss of habitat and because they are the most illegally trafficked species in the world. They live in Africa and Asia.

The **platypus** (*Ornithorhynchus anatinus*) is one of the few species of mammals that lay eggs. It eats insect larvae, shrimp, and crayfish. It is only found in Australia.

The **saiga antelope** (*Saiga tatarica*) is found in one part of Russia and three different areas of Kazakhstan. Its nose filters dust from the herd, cools the air when the temperature is high, and heats the air when it's cold. It eats herbs, grass, and shrubs.

The **star-nosed mole** (*Condylura cristata*) is found in northern parts of North America. It uses its sensitive nose to locate underground prey such as worms and grubs.

The **Sunda flying lemur** (*Galeopterus variegatus*) is a cobego and not a lemur. It is found throughout Southeast Asia. It does not fly, but glides with flaps of skin attached to outstretched limbs. It eats leaves, fruit, coconut flowers, and sap.

The **thorny dragon** (*Moloch horridus*) is a lizard common to Australian deserts. Sharp spiny thorns protect it from predators. It collects water through its skin.

Glossary

amphibians: one of the most well-known classes of animals includes frogs and salamanders.

birds: one of the most well-known classes of animals includes robins, ducks, and chickens.

camouflage: hide or disguise.

cobego: a mammal that lives in trees and looks like a lemur.

crocodilian: a reptile in a group that includes alligators, crocodiles, and the gharial.

fish: one of the most well-known classes of animals includes cod, guppies, and goldfish.

insects: a group of small six-legged animals that includes ants, bees, and butterflies.

larvae: young insects that are very different from the adults.

lizard: a type of reptile.

mammals: one of the most well-known classes of animals includes cats, dogs, and humans.

predator: an animal that eats another animal.

prey: an animal that is eaten by another animal.

proboscis: a mouthpart that many insects have for eating.

reptiles: one of the most well-known classes of animals includes alligators and snakes.

Scyphozoa: a class of animals that includes jellyfish.

spiders: a group of small wingless, eight-legged animals that includes the American house spider and daddy longlegs.

Bibliography

Books

Bessette, Alan E., William K. Capman. *Plants and Flowers*. New York: Dover, 1992

Clement, Roland C. *The Living World of Audubon*. New York: Simon and Schuster, 1974

Grasse, P. P. *Larousse Animal Portraits*. New York: Larousse, 1977

Harter, Jim. *Animal: 1,419 Copyright-Free Illustrations of Mammals, Birds, Fish, Insects, Etc.* New York: Dover, 1979

Heck, J. G. *Heck's Pictorial Archive of Nature and Science*. New York: Dover, 1994

Leclerc, comte de Buffon, Georges-Louis. *368 Animal Illustrations from Buffon's "Natural History."* New York: Dover, 1993

Olsen, Roberta J. M. *Audubon's Aviary*. New York: Rizzoli, 2012

Websites

https://www.britannica.com/

https://www.nationalgeographic.com/animals

https://www.nature.com/

https://www.wildlifetrusts.org/